Spelling Two

An Interactive Vocabulary & Spelling Workbook for 6-Year-Olds.

(With AudioBook Lessons)

By

Bukky Ekine-Ogunlana

Published by
TCEC Publishing

Table of Contents

Table of Contents

Dedication

This book is dedicated to our three exceptional children and all the beautiful children worldwide who have passed through the T.C.E.C 6-16 years program over the years. Thank you for the opportunity to serve you and invest in your colourful and bright future.

Introduction

A re you ready to get to the next milestone?

Spelling two is the second Spelling for Kids series book and will cover 264 words.

It is ideal for six-year-olds. It's up to you to hear them, understand them, learn their spelling, and finally, learn to write them down correctly.

If you follow the instructions I have already given you, it will be a piece of cake! Remember first to hear the word, then read it in the sentence, write it down, and check its spelling.

You can do it as often as possible to ensure you fully grasp each word and remember its spelling.

Practice makes perfect, after all.

So...on your marks, get set, go!

Spelling 2-1

1. Spell:

Lexie will _____ you

some of her crayons for your

coloring.

2. Spell:

Tyler_____

his drink to his sister.

3. Spell:

_____ still so

that we can take a photo.

Spelling 2-1

4. Spell:

_____ this dress suit

me?

5. Spell:

Beth has a _____

bag.

6. Spell:

The school bus _____

had already before we

finished breakfast.

Spelling 2-1

7. Spell:

Kitty got a _____

ticket for the show.

8. Spell:

Rose has a pink _____

for her birthday.

9. Spell:

The entrance

_____ is open.

Spelling 2-1

10. Spell:

Callum had a cup of _____

with biscuits.

11. Spell:

_____Tom, it's been a long

time since your last visit, and I

want to know if you are well.

12. Spell:

I can not _____ my

pencil.

That's it for lesson 1... So you can enjoy the rest of your fantastic day!

Spelling 2-2

I. Spell:

I _____ my mum

driving off the driveway.

2. Spell:

I am _____ that

I got all my sums right.

3. Spell:

I tried my _____

in the timetabling challenge

today.

Spelling 2-2

4. Spell:

_____ of my friends is

going to the hospital today.

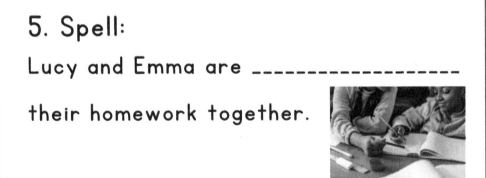

5. Spell:

Lucy and Emma are _____

their homework together.

6. Spell:

I will be _____

swimming on Saturday.

Spelling 2-2

7. Spell:

There are seven days in a

---------------------.

Sun
Mon
Tue
Wed
Thu
Fri
Sat

8. Spell:

I gave the dog a --------------------

to chew.

9. Spell:

My birthday party will

------------------- a lot

of money.

Spelling 2-2

10. Spell:
The rocket disappeared in the

_____ soon

after taking off.

11. Spell:
My family is going

_____ on

holiday to Dubai.

12. Spell:
Dylan _____

seven years old.

Congrats! You have finished learning the words in lesson 2. Remember to know and understand the meaning of all the new words you have found.

Spelling 2-3

1. Spell:

There are _____

questions in the spelling test.

2. Spell:

I got 12 questions out

_____ the 12

questions in the assessment.

3. Spell:

I _____ a lot of

vegetables with my rice.

Spelling 2-3

4. Spell:

My mother tells me a

_____ before

I fall asleep.

5. Spell:

The Headteacher gave us a

_____ time to

play because we were naughty.

6. Spell:

I like bacon _____

my eggs.

Spelling 2-3

7. Spell:
Jude will _____

you some money for your

transport.

8. Spell:
We bought a _____

of bread for our breakfast.

9. Spell:
The School choir will sing

_____ the

hall.

Spelling 2-3

10. Spell:

The best _____

to do is apologize to him.

11. Spell:

I have never _____

anyone his secret.

12. Spell:

I _____ my brother

to come to my school.

You've made it! You completed lesson 3. Pay attention, kids; if you find it difficult to learn some words, you should write them down on paper. That will help you remember them better.

Spelling 2-4

1. Spell:

Tommy will _____

his football lessons on Sunday.

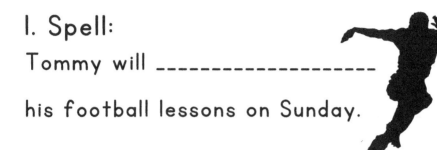

2. Spell:

Are _____

the drawings you made at

school?

3. Spell:

_____ swimming in

the sea, we built castles

in the sand.

spelling 2-4

4. Spell:
Anthony walked

_____ the

road to get some drinks.

5. Spell:
I am making a jam sandwich

for _____ .

6. Spell:
The children _____

sitting quietly in the room.

Spelling 2-4

7. Spell:

Amelia will be _____

to my house on Sunday.

8. Spell:

The _____ is green.

9. Spell:

We will _____ the

classroom tidy.

Spelling 2-4

10. Spell:
She said the same thing

---------------------- .

11. Spell:
Come on and

-------------------- my day,

Tim! Tell me some good news.

12. Spell:
Daniel did _____

the ball into the road.

Great! Lesson 4 is over! I suggest you get some rest before going on to the next lesson. That will help you recharge and return to the next task more refreshed! Great work!

Spelling 2-5

1. Spell:

You can _____your

eyes now and search for

the hideout.

2. Spell:

There are many pencils

_____ my

pencil case.

3. Spell:

I _____ a tuna

sandwich with my mum.

Spelling 2-5

4. Spell:

Jesse has only one

_____.

5. Spell:

Aaron had an _____

sandwich for two days

in a roll.

6. Spell:

What are we having for

_____, mom?

Spelling 2-5

7. Spell:

The cheetah can run

---------------------.

8. Spell:

My dad works every day from

nine to _____.

9. Spell:

Joe _____ second

in the long jump.

Spelling 2-5

10. Spell:

Tracy put an

_____ pack on

her swollen finger.

11. Spell:

My sister is three years

_____.

12. Spell:

The new-born did

_____ for her mum.

Fantastic! You have finished the words in lesson 5. What a task! Kids, keep a note: An easy way to learn the majority of new words is to break them apart; in that way, the words can be easily organized from the shortest to the longest.

Spelling 2-6

1. Spell:

Ella was the

------------------- girl to

win the contest ever.

WIN

2. Spell:

The -------------------

whistled when it arrived at

the station.

3. Spell:

------------------- is taking

Alfie to his guitar lesson?

Spelling 2-6

4. Spell:

Never cross the

_____ before

first from both sides.

5. Spell:

_____ is necessary

for life on the planet.

6. Spell:

Karen is an old _____ of

my brother.

Spelling 2-6

7. Spell:

Wearing a seat belt keeps you

_____ in case of a

car accident.

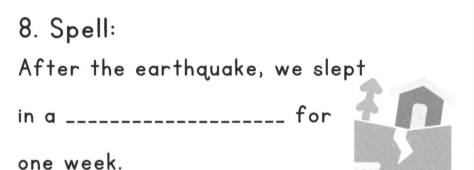

8. Spell:

After the earthquake, we slept

in a _____ for

one week.

9. Spell:

Abigail did _____ a

boat in the race.

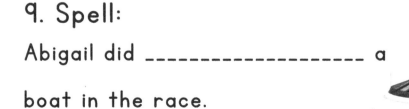

Spelling 2-6

10. Spell:

It will be _____ if you

can come to my brother's

wedding.

11. Spell:

Daniel put the bird in the

white _____ .

12. Spell:

Oliver has a round _____

with freckles.

Lesson 6 has come to an end. Awesome! Keep up the excellent work! And do not forget: Repetition makes the master!

Spelling 2-7

1. Spell:

The teenager helped the old lady

----

her shopping trolley.

2. Spell:

She played a _____

on him.

3. Spell:

------------------- you coming

along with me?

Spelling 2-7

4. Spell:
Ben was not _____

his work in class, so I told the

teacher.

5. Spell:

_____ of my

friends are going to the

dance tomorrow.

6. Spell:
We have a new _____

in our kitchen.

Spelling 2-7

7. Spell:

The _____ says

seven o'clock.

8. Spell:

I can _____

the road on my own.

9. Spell:

I have _____

brothers.

Spelling 2-7

10. Spell:

I had an _____ with my

breakfast.

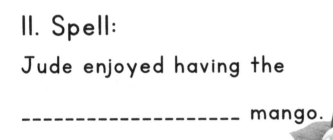

11. Spell:

Jude enjoyed having the

_____ mango.

12. Spell:

With _____ and butter,

you can make your breakfast.

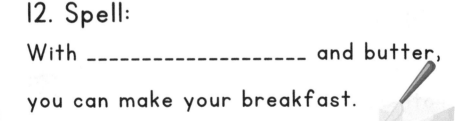

Look at how far you have gone! You have reached and completed lesson 7! What a student you are!
Congratulations!

Spelling 2-8

I. Spell:

Ella will _____

my hair when she comes.

2. Spell:

The _____ is full of

water.

3. Spell:

We had a fun lesson with Mrs. Smith

in _____

today.

Spelling 2-8

4. Spell:

Elizabeth goes to _____

with her family every Sunday.

5. Spell:

Julius was _____ when

he heard that his parents

were breaking up.

6. Spell:

They interrupted the program to

report a breaking

_____.

Spelling 2-8

7. Spell:

Molly walks about a

_____ to

school every day.

8. Spell:

Billy pushed the shopping

_____ for

his grandmother.

9. Spell:

The _____ loaded

the cart with tomatoes.

Spelling 2-8

10. Spell:

The back _____ has

lovely flowers.

11. Spell:

Granddad looked after the

_____ while we

went away on holiday.

12. Spell:

Dark clouds always bring

_____ .

Look at you! You are natural! And it seems that you will be a spelling bee master
pretty soon! You have just finished lesson 8.

Spelling 2-9

1. Spell:

A _____ has

four legs.

2. Spell:

The _____ girl

was timid.

3. Spell:

I will _____ my mum if

you can come for a

sleepover today.

Spelling 2-9

4. Spell:

After the sunset, the stars appeared

in the _____ .

5. Spell:

Lily threatened to

_____ the

wood house down.

6. Spell:

I like my mummy

_____ daddy.

Spelling 2-9

7. Spell:

Buying a _____

coat can be very expensive.

8. Spell:

Megan got a new

_____ pencil

case.

9. Spell:

Sheila will

_____ the

water in her water bottle.

Spelling 2-9

10. Spell:

Tina was _____ to

the old lady by standing up for

her on the bus.

11. Spell:

He left the front door open,

and the cat was

_____ .

12. Spell:

I bought this doll during the

sale at _____

price.

Well done! You have finished lesson 9. You should be proud of yourself! And
remember this: Always enunciate each word properly; this method will help you
spell the word correctly.

Spelling 2-10

1. Spell:

Keep your _____

up to look more confident.

2. Spell:

Tom poured his drink into a

_____ cup.

3. Spell:

Teddy polished his pair of

_____ with his

grandad.

Spelling 2-10

4. Spell:

The test will _____

after an hour.

5. Spell:

You should _____

saving money to buy a car.

6. Spell:

Bella found it hard to stir the

_____

soup.

Spelling 2-10

7. Spell:

Lucy has bought her train

_____ for

the trip.

8. Spell:

Come on, _____

! Get on that dance floor!

9. Spell:

My dad has enough

_____ to pay for a

new car.

Spelling 2-10

10. Spell:
Doing spelling exercises helps you

_____ your

spelling skills.

11. Spell:
The _____ shook

hands with everyone in the

match.

12. Spell:
If you want a _____

lunch, buy a sandwich.

You completed lesson 10! Bravo! You are doing a great job. Pretty soon, you will be an expert in spelling.

Spelling 2-11

1. Spell:

The Headteacher will be spending the

_____ term in

a new school.

2. Spell:

Bob wears two jumpers during the

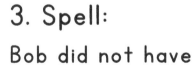 _____ months.

3. Spell:

Bob did not have

_____ money

on him.

Spelling 2-11

4. Spell:

Ben is not good at

_____ animals,

but he paints them well.

5. Spell:

How _____ rulers

are in your pencil case?

6. Spell:

The little girl did

_____ under

the table.

Spelling 2-11

7. Spell:

Sue wore a _____

dress for the choir rehearsal.

8. Spell:

Bill is going _____

next week to New York.

9. Spell:

Ted is now _____

confident in his two-times table

after much practice.

Spelling 2-11

10. Spell:

Anthony is wearing a red cap on

his _____ .

11. Spell:

Jude was able to _____

the secret box.

12. Spell:

I will _____

my parents my report card

after school.

Great work! You have completed lesson 11.

Spelling 2-12

1. Spell:

Mr. Oliver had to _____

because all the seats

were taken on the train.

2. Spell:

Jane can _____ her

dog.

3. Spell:

She came to the shop

_____ midday.

Spelling 2-12

4. Spell:

I _____ I should domy

spelling right away.

5. Spell:

I did _____ in my spelling

at school after practicing at

home with my spelling book.

6. Spell:

He fell _____

as soon as his face touched

the pillow.

Spelling 2-12

7. Spell:

We _____ the hidden

treasure with the help of

this old map.

8. Spell:

The teacher asked the class to

_____ up the

mess on the floor.

9. Spell:

The bus for the excursion was

_____

of people.

Spelling 2-12

10. Spell:

There are lots of red cars on

the _____.

11. Spell:

Mr. Philip told the class an exciting

_____ .

12. Spell:

The school dinner is going to be

yummy on _____.

You have done a great job finishing words in lesson 12. With this rhythm, you are about to be a master in spelling soon.

Spelling 2-13

1. Spell:

Every Sunday we go for a picnic at

the _ _ _ _ _ _ _ _ _ _ _ _ _ _ _ _ _ _ .

2. Spell:

Tonight's _ _ _ _ _ _ _ _ _ _ _ _ _ _ _ _ _ _

is a popular TV series.

3. Spell:

Loretta loves her

_ _ _ _ _ _ _ _ _ _ _ _ _ _ _ _ _ dolly.

Spelling 2-13

4. Spell:

Jane helped her mum

------------------- the

dishes.

5. Spell:

The school uniform is a grey

------------------- and a

white blouse.

6. Spell:

I brush my teeth every

------------------- after

having breakfast.

Spelling 2-13

7. Spell:

A massive _____ of

smoke came from the factory.

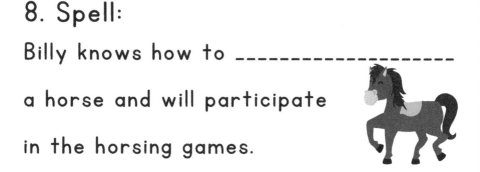

8. Spell:

Billy knows how to _____

a horse and will participate

in the horsing games.

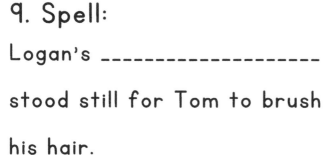

9. Spell:

Logan's _____

stood still for Tom to brush

his hair.

Spelling 2-13

10. Spell:

Mr. Fisher does not trust

_____ in the

class.

11. Spell:

That was the worst score that

I have _____ had

on any test.

12. Spell:

I will _____ be

rude to my teachers.

Congrats! You have made such Progress! You finished the words in lesson 13 already. Don't forget to practice new vocabulary every week. First, learn the meaning of the word and the spelling of it. Then surprise everyone with your spelling skills.

Spelling 2-14

1. Spell:
The cat kept _____

at the lady.

2. Spell:
The toy store is right after

the _____ of

the road.

3. Spell:
The _____

alarm in the room is not

working.

Spelling 2-14

4. Spell:

You need _____ to

make a cake.

5. Spell:

We are going to _____

some money at the beach

on ice lollies.

6. Spell:

Fishes live in the

_____ .

Spelling 2-14

7. Spell:

_____ are twenty

children in our class.

8. Spell:

Benny could not keep

_____ after

9 pm.

9. Spell:

_____ was Nathan's

christening.

Spelling 2-14

10. Spell:

_____ is your

name?

11. Spell:

Where is _____

spelling book?

12. Spell:

Ella is going to her dance

lesson on _____.

What progress! You completed lesson 14 already. You should be proud of yourself!

Spelling 2-15

1. Spell:

Billy can drive a big

------------------------ .

2. Spell:

The --------------------- clothes

are in the washing machine.

3. Spell:

The lesson ends at

-------------------- o'clock.

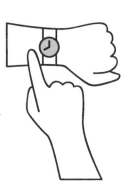

Spelling 2-15

4. Spell:

I am Sam; what's your

_____ ?

5. Spell:

_____ is Monday.

6. Spell:

The baby will not

_____ if you

take his toy away.

Spelling 2-15

7. Spell:

She took a _____

with her Nanny.

8. Spell:

The dog is _____

old, and he cannot hear well.

9. Spell:

Denis heard _____

talking in the next room.

Spelling 2-15

10. Spell:

What is _____

name?

11. Spell:

_____ is bothering

me in this situation, but I can

not tell what exactly.

12. Spell:

Alfie is going for his football

training on _____

Wonderful! You have completed words in lesson 15. Keep up the excellent work, and don't forget: Words matter, and most importantly, correctly written words matter.

Spelling 2-16

I. Spell:

Joseph crossed the _ _ _ _ _ _ _ _ _ _ _ _ _ _ _ _ _ _

with his mummy.

2. Spell:

Hey Mark, come _ _ _ _ _ _ _ _ _ _ _ _ _ _ _ _ _ _ _

with me to play football.

3. Spell:

The soldiers _ _ _ _ _ _ _ _ _ _ _ _ _ _ _ _ _

up in rows for the military

parade.

Spelling 2-16

4. Spell:

_____ names

are on the class register.

5. Spell:
The old lady called

_____ for help.

6. Spell:
Jude and James are going to

a _____ party

on Saturday.

Spelling 2-16

7. Spell:

Jesus _____

on the cross for all our sins.

8. Spell:

There are twelve months in a

_____ .

9. Spell:

My mom wears earplugs when she sleeps

because she doesn't want to

_____ dad snoring.

Spelling 2-16

10. Spell:

Always _____ your

bike with your helmet on.

11. Spell:

Jake did not _____

his sentence with a full stop.

12. Spell:

The carpenter came to

_____ the

broken table.

You have done a great job finishing words in lesson 16. With this rhythm, you are about to be a master in spelling soon.

Spelling 2-17

I. Spell:

Can you spell your

_____ ,please?

2. Spell:

What do you want to use the

pencil _____ ?

3. Spell:

I will keep my promise, and I will

never _____ you.

Spelling 2-17

4. Spell:

The Snow Queen wore a

_____ gown.

5. Spell:

The cowboy threw a

_____ to catch

the cow.

6. Spell:

Julia could not go out

_____ it was

raining.

Spelling 2-17

7. Spell:

The chair is _____

the table.

8. Spell:

My gran grew the

_____ flower

in her garden.

9. Spell:

The _____ conditioner

is on, so we have a low

temperature in the house.

Spelling 2-17

10. Spell:
She opened the

_____ to get

some fresh air into the room.

11. Spell:
My older brother worked as a

lifeguard last

_____ .

12. Spell:
You always fight like a cat

and _____ .

Fantastic! You have completed spelling lesson 17! You're almost done.

Spelling 2-18

1. Spell:
Jude forgot to mail his

_____ the

letter.

2. Spell:
The boys have _____

to school.

3. Spell:
Daniel is _____

to the match on Saturday.

Spelling 2-18

4. Spell:

David spoke clearly and confidently

in _____

of the whole class.

5. Spell:

It's _____

outside; it seems that it is

going to snow.

6. Spell:

_____ is the

time to keep quiet.

Spelling 2-18

7. Spell:

I will never _____ my

dad's advice.

8. Spell:

Who is _____ for

vaccination?

9. Spell:

_____ Balance is a

popular sneakers trademark.

Spelling 2-18

10. Spell:

The swimming instructor will

_____ him out

of the pool.

11. Spell:

_____ tea is

served at 5:00 pm.

12. Spell:

Seize the _____ and

make the best of it.

You are doing so well! You have completed words in spelling lesson 18. Bravo!

Spelling 2-19

1. Spell:
Elizabeth got a new piano for her

_____ presents.

2. Spell:

_____ before you

speak.

3. Spell:
There is a _____

fountain in the school playground.

Spelling 2-19

4. Spell:

My _____ plays

football and Rugby.

5. Spell:

Five is more

_____ two.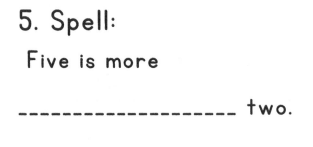

6. Spell:

I walk to school on

_____ .

Spelling 2-19

7. Spell:

He offered me his _____

to sit because I felt dizzy.

8. Spell:

I drew a rose _____

for my mum on mother's day.

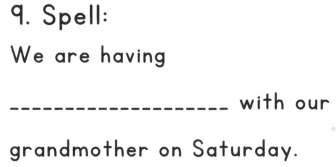

9. Spell:

We are having

_____ with our

grandmother on Saturday.

Spelling 2-19

10. Spell:

The house where I grew up is

_____ of my

childhood memories.

11. Spell:

All the girls wore _____

uniforms to school.

12. Spell:

_____ is the

sheep's hair, and it keeps

them very warm.

You have finished the words in lesson 19. Fantastic!

Spelling 2-20

I. Spell:

_____ your life to the

fullest!

2. Spell:

It will _____ you

lesser money if you buy it o

sales.

3. Spell:

Billy rode his _____

on Sunday.

Spelling 2-20

4. Spell:

Billy _____ his wallet

at the playground.

5. Spell:

I like to _____

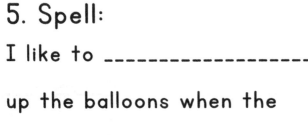

up the balloons when the

party is over.

6. Spell:

I will start to draw the cat on a new

_____ .

Spelling 2-20

7. Spell:

Steven won the _____

medal.

8. Spell:

Ella wrote a _____

to her penfriend in Germany.

9. Spell:

Luke was _____ in

confronting the bully in

his class.

Spelling 2-20

10. Spell:

_____ you pass me

the salt, please?

11. Spell:

Kitty _____ be

practicing her spelling instead of

singing. Spelling

12. Spell:

The baby _____

cry if you tease him.

Spelling lesson 20 is over. You finished it and, more importantly, learned the lesson's words. However, if you have doubts about one or more words, do not worry; return to the word and make as many revisions as necessary.

Spelling 2-21

I. Spell:

Ben wore a white _____

for the occasion.

2. Spell:

My mum bought me

_____ pair of

trainers.

3. Spell:

_____ night is

pizza night for this family.

Spelling 2-21

4. Spell:

We _____ all be

taking part in the drama.

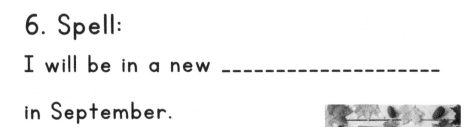

5. Spell:

My uncle and his wife had a good view

of the _____ .

6. Spell:

I will be in a new _____

in September.

Spelling 2-21

7. Spell:

The teacher advised my sister to

read _____ books.

8. Spell:

The teacher allowed the students to

have a _____

break.

9. Spell:

The older man left the

_____ last week.

Spelling 2-21

10. Spell:

I can hear you very well, and

you don't have to

_____ !

11. Spell:

In _____ , the flowers

blossom.

12. Spell:

We learned how to write an

informative _____

today at school.

Excellent work, kid! You have made it! You are so close to the end. Lesson 21 is
complete. One more task is left, and you are done with spelling 2. Right? Okay,
let's go!

Spelling 2-22

1. Spell:

Sanjay bought a new pair of

_____ trainers.

2. Spell:

Let's play _____

and seek.

3. Spell:

The ball is

_____ the

table.

Spelling 2-22

4. Spell:
The pencil is _____.

5. Spell:
The _____ was locked, but

the thief managed to break

the lock and get into the house.

6. Spell:
Magdalene is a

_____ friend.

Spelling 2-22

7. Spell:

Ted dropped the letter in the

_____ .

8. Spell:

Jude will go to his swimming

lessons on

_____ .

9. Spell:

_____ student must

have a student card.

Spelling 2-22

10. Spell:

Did you _____ the noise

that came from the garden?

11. Spell:

The class teacher gave us a

_____ each for

being sensible in the school choir.

12. Spell:

Mary looks good in

_____ colors.

Conclusion

CONGRATULATIONS, you little spelling champions!

You have finally finished Spelling 2!

Well done! Do you hear the trumpets sound?

Well, I do! And you should take pride in yourself. And the same goes for your guardians, parents, or teacher!

By now, you should be capable of spelling 264 more new words. Two hundred and sixty-four new words are added to your vocabulary. Boy, isn't that a small triumph?

I bet you already feel more confident in your spelling skills. However, don't get too much confidence though. Remember to make the necessary revisions to ensure you know the words' dictation and meaning. And if by any chance some words seem to bother you, focus on them by repeating the practice. Repetition makes the master; don't you ever forget that.

Our next appointment is with Spelling 3.
See you there!

Please leave a 1-click Review!

I would be incredibly thankful if you could take just 60 seconds to write a brief review on Amazon or the platform of purchase, even if it's just a few sentences!

Answers

Spelling 2-1

1. Spell: <u>Give</u>
2. Spell: <u>Gave</u>
3. Spell: <u>Stand</u>
4. Spell: <u>Does</u>
5. Spell: <u>Small</u>
6. Spell: <u>Gone</u>
7. Spell: <u>Free</u>
8. Spell: <u>Cake</u>
9. Spell: <u>Door</u>
10. Spell: <u>Tea</u>
11. Spell: <u>Dear</u>
12. Spell: <u>Find</u>

Spelling 2-2

1. Spell: <u>Saw</u>
2. Spell: <u>Happy</u>
3. Spell: <u>Best</u>
4. Spell: <u>One</u>
5. Spell: <u>Doing</u>
6. Spell: <u>Going</u>
7. Spell: <u>Week</u>
8. Spell: <u>Bone</u>
9. Spell: <u>Cost</u>
10. Spell: <u>Sky</u>
11. Spell: <u>Away</u>
12. Spell: <u>Is</u>

Answers

Spelling 2-3

1. Spell: <u>Nine</u>

2. Spell: <u>Of</u>

3. Spell: <u>Eat</u>

4. Spell: <u>Story</u>

5. Spell: <u>Short</u>

6. Spell: <u>With</u>

7. Spell: <u>Give</u>

8. Spell: <u>Loaf</u>

9. Spell: <u>At</u>

10. Spell: <u>Thing</u>

11. Spell: <u>Told</u>

12. Spell: <u>Want</u>

Spelling 2-4

1. Spell: <u>Stop</u>

2. Spell: <u>These</u>

3. Spell: <u>After</u>

4. Spell: <u>Down</u>

5. Spell: <u>Myself</u>

6. Spell: <u>Were</u>

7. Spell: <u>Coming</u>

8. Spell: <u>Leaf</u>

9. Spell: <u>Keep</u>

10. Spell: <u>Again</u>

11. Spell: <u>Make</u>

12. Spell: <u>Kick</u>

Answers

Spelling 2-5

1.Spell: <u>Open</u>

2.Spell: <u>Inside</u>

3.Spell: <u>Made</u>

4.Spell: <u>Sister</u>

5.Spell: <u>Egg</u>

6.Spell: <u>Dinner</u>

7.Spell: <u>Fast</u>

8.Spell: <u>Five</u>

9.Spell: <u>Came</u>.

10.Spell: <u>Ice</u>

11.Spell: <u>Old</u>

12.Spell: <u>Cry_</u>

Spelling 2- 6

1.Spell: <u>First</u>

2.Spell: <u>Train</u>

3.Spell: <u>Who</u>

4.Spell: <u>Street</u>

5.Spell: <u>Water</u> .

6.Spell: <u>Mate</u>

7.Spell: <u>Safe</u>

8.Spell: <u>Tent</u>

9.Spell: Sai l

10.Spell: <u>Nice</u>

11.Spell: <u>Cage</u>

12.Spell: <u>Face</u>

Answers

Spelling 2-7

1. Spell: <u>Push</u>

2. Spell: <u>Trick</u>

3. Spell: <u>Are</u>

4. Spell: <u>Doing</u>

5. Spell: <u>Many</u>

6. Spell: <u>Clock</u>

7. Spell: <u>Time</u>

8. Spell: <u>Cross</u>

9. Spell: <u>Two</u>

10. Spell: <u>Apple</u>

11. Spell: <u>Ripe</u>

12. Spell: <u>Bread</u>

Spelling 2- 8

1. Spell: <u>Brush</u>

2. Spell: <u>Bucket</u>

3. Spell: <u>Class</u>

4. Spell: <u>Church</u>

5. Spell: <u>Hurt</u>

6. Spell: <u>News</u>

7. Spell: <u>Mile</u>

8. Spell: <u>Cart</u>

9. Spell: <u>Farmer</u>

10. Spell: <u>Garden</u>

11. Spell: <u>Kitten</u>

12. Spell: <u>Rain</u>

Answers

Spelling 2-9

1.Spell: <u>Table</u>

2.Spell: <u>New</u>

3.Spell: <u>Ask</u>

4.Spell: <u>Sky</u>

5.Spell: <u>Burn</u>

6.Spell: <u>And</u>

7.Spell: <u>Fur</u>

8.Spell: <u>Brown</u>

9.Spell: <u>Drink</u>

10.Spell: <u>Kind</u>

11.Spell: <u>Gone</u>

12.Spell: <u>Half</u>

Spelling 2- 10

1.Spell: <u>Head</u>

2.Spell: <u>Clean</u>

3.Spell: <u>Shoes</u>

4.Spell: <u>Stop</u>

5.Spell: <u>Begin</u>

6.Spell: <u>Thick</u>

7.Spell: <u>Ticket</u>

8.Spell:<u>Everybody</u>

9.Spell: <u>Money</u>

10.Spell: <u>Improve</u>

11.Spell: <u>Queen</u>

12.Spell: <u>Quick</u>

Answers

Spelling 2-11

1. Spell: <u>Summer</u>
2. Spell: <u>Winter</u>
3. Spell: <u>Any</u>
4. Spell: <u>Drawing</u>
5. Spell: <u>Many</u>
6. Spell: <u>Hide</u>
7. Spell: <u>Yellow</u>
8. Spell: <u>Away</u>
9. Spell: <u>Very</u>
10. Spell: <u>Head</u>
11. Spell: <u>Open</u>
12. Spell: <u>Show</u>

Spelling 2-12

1. Spell: <u>Stand</u>
2. Spell: <u>Bathe</u>
3. Spell: <u>Around</u>
4. Spell: <u>Think</u>
5. Spell: <u>Better</u>
6. Spell: <u>Asleep</u>
7. Spell: <u>Found</u>
8. Spell: <u>Clean</u>
9. Spell: <u>Ful l</u>
10. Spell: <u>Road</u>
11. Spell: <u>Story</u>
12. Spell: <u>Tuesday</u>

Answers

Spelling 2-13

1. Spell: <u>Park</u>
2. Spell: <u>Show</u>
3. Spell: <u>Pink</u>
4. Spell: <u>Wash</u>
5. Spell: <u>Skirt</u>
6. Spell: <u>Morning</u>
7. Spell: <u>Cloud</u>
8. Spell: <u>Ride</u>
9. Spell: <u>Horse</u>
10. Spell: <u>Anyone</u>
11. Spell: <u>Ever</u>
12. Spell: <u>Never</u>

Spelling 2- 14

1. Spell: <u>Staring</u>
2. Spell: <u>Corner</u>
3. Spell: <u>Smoke</u>
4. Spell: <u>Butter</u>
5. Spell: <u>Spend</u>
6. Spell: <u>Sea</u>
7. Spell: <u>There</u>
8. Spell: <u>Awake</u>
9. Spell: <u>Yesterday</u>
10. Spell: <u>What</u>
11. Spell: <u>Your</u>
12. Spell: <u>Wednesday</u>

Answers

Spelling 2-15

1. Spell: <u>Truck</u>
2. Spell: <u>Dirty</u>
3. Spell: <u>Three</u>
4. Spell: <u>Name</u>
5. Spell: <u>Today</u>
6. Spell: <u>Cry</u>
7. Spell: <u>Walk</u>
8. Spell: <u>Very</u>
9. Spell: <u>Someone</u>
10. Spell: <u>His</u>
11. Spell: <u>Something</u>
12. Spell: <u>Thursday</u>

Spelling 2- 16

1. Spell: <u>Road</u>
2. Spell: <u>Along</u>
3. Spell: <u>Lined</u>
4. Spell: <u>Our</u>
5. Spell: <u>Out</u>
6. Spell: <u>Beach</u>
7. Spell: <u>Died</u>
8. Spell: <u>Year</u>
9. Spell: <u>Hear</u>
10. Spell: <u>Ride</u>
11. Spell: <u>End</u>
12. Spell: <u>Fix</u>

Answers

Spelling 2-17

1. Spell: <u>Name</u>
2. Spell: <u>For</u>
3. Spell: <u>Cross</u>
4. Spell: <u>White</u>
5. Spell: <u>Rope</u>
6. Spell: <u>Because</u>
7. Spell: <u>Beside</u>
8. Spell: <u>Rose</u>
9. Spell: <u>Air</u>
10. Spell: <u>Window</u>
11. Spell: <u>Summer</u>
12. Spell: <u>Mouse</u>

Spelling 2- 18

1. Spell: <u>Father</u>
2. Spell: <u>Gone</u>
3. Spell: <u>Coming</u>
4. Spell: <u>Front</u>
5. Spell: <u>Cold</u>
6. Spell: <u>Now</u>
7. Spell: <u>Forget</u>
8. Spell: <u>Next</u>
9. Spell: <u>New</u>
10. Spell: <u>Pull</u>
11. Spell: <u>Afternoon</u>
12. Spell: <u>Day</u>

Answers

Spelling 2-19

1. Spell: <u>Christmas</u>
2. Spell: <u>Think</u>
3. Spell: <u>Water</u>
4. Spell: <u>Brother</u>
5. Spell: <u>Than</u>
6. Spell: <u>Foot</u>
7. Spell: <u>Chair</u>
8. Spell: <u>Flower</u>
9. Spell: <u>Lunch</u>
10. Spell: <u>Full</u>
11. Spell: <u>Their</u>
12. Spell: <u>Wool</u>

Spelling 2- 20

1. Spell: <u>Live</u>
2. Spell: <u>Cost</u>
3. Spell: <u>Horse</u>
4. Spell: <u>Lost</u>
5. Spell: <u>Blow</u>
6. Spell: <u>Page</u>
7. Spell: <u>Gold</u>
8. Spell: <u>Letter</u>
9. Spell: <u>Brave</u>
10. Spell: <u>Could</u>
11. Spell: <u>Should</u>
12. Spell: <u>Would</u>

Answers

Spelling 2-21

1. Spell: <u>Shirt</u>

2. Spell: <u>Another</u>

3. Spell: <u>Friday</u>

4. Spell: <u>Will</u>

5. Spell: <u>Creek</u>

6. Spell: <u>Class</u>

7. Spell: <u>Those</u>

8. Spell: <u>Short</u>

9. Spell: <u>Town</u>

10. Spell: <u>Shout</u>

11. Spell: <u>Spring</u>

12. Spell: <u>Letter</u>

Spelling 2- 22

1. Spell: <u>White</u>

2. Spell: <u>Hide</u>

3. Spell: <u>Under</u>

4. Spell: <u>Sharp</u>

5. Spell: <u>Door</u>

6. Spell: <u>Nice</u>

7. Spell: <u>Mail</u>

8. Spell: <u>Monday</u>

9. Spell: <u>Each</u>

10. Spell: <u>Hear</u>

11. Spell: <u>Sweet</u>

12. Spell: <u>Those</u>

Other Books You'll Love!

1. **Spelling one: An Interactive Vocabulary & Spelling**

   Workbook for 5-Year-Olds. *(With Audiobook Lessons)*

2. **Spelling Two: An Interactive Vocabulary & Spelling**

   Workbook for 6-Year-Olds. *(With Audiobook Lessons)*

3. **Spelling Three: An Interactive Vocabulary & Spelling**

   Workbook for 7-Year-Olds. *(With Audiobook Lessons)*

4. **Spelling Four: An Interactive Vocabulary & Spelling**

   Workbook for 8-Year-Olds. *(With Audiobook Lessons)*

5. **Spelling Five: An Interactive Vocabulary & Spelling**

   Workbook for 9-Year-Olds. *(With Audiobook Lessons)*

6. **Spelling Six: An Interactive Vocabulary & Spelling**

   Workbook for 10 & 11 Years Old. *(With Audiobook Lessons)*

7. **Spelling Seven: An Interactive Vocabulary & Spelling**

   Workbook for 12-14 Years-Old. *(With Audiobook Lessons)*

Other Books You'll Love!

8. Raising Boys in Today's Digital World:
Proven Positive Parenting Tips for Raising Respectful, Successful, and Confident Boys

9. Raising Girls in Today's Digital World:
Proven Positive Parenting Tips for Raising Respectful, Successful, and Confident Girls

10. Raising Kids in Today's Digital World:
Proven Positive Parenting Tips for Raising Respectful, Successful, and Confident Kids

11. The Child Development and Positive Parenting Master Class 2-in-1 Bundle:
Proven Methods for Raising Well-Behaved and Intelligent Children, with Accelerated Learning Methods

12. Parenting Teens in Today's Challenging World 2-in-1 Bundle:
Proven Methods for Improving Teenager's Behaviour with Positive Parenting and Family Communication

13. Life Strategies for Teenagers:
Positive Parenting, Tips and Understanding Teens for Better Communication and a Happy Family

14. Parenting Teen Girls in Today's Challenging World:
Proven Methods for Improving Teenager's Behaviour with Whole Brain Training

Other Books You'll Love!

15. Parenting Teen Boys in Today's Challenging World:
Proven Methods for Improving Teenager's Behaviour with Whole Brain Training

16. 101 Tips For Helping With Your Child's Learning:
Proven Strategies for Accelerated Learning and Raising Smart Children Using Positive Parenting Skills

17. 101 Tips for Child Development:
 Proven Methods for Raising Children and Improving Kids Behavior with Whole Brain Training

18. Financial Tips to Help Kids:
Proven Methods for Teaching Kids Money Management and Financial Responsibility

19. Healthy Habits for Kids:
 Positive Parenting Tips for Fun Kids Exercises, Healthy Snacks, and Improved Kids Nutrition

20. Mini Habits for Happy Kids:
Proven Parenting Tips for Positive Discipline and Improving Kids' Behavior

21. Good Habits for Healthy Kids 2-in-1 Combo Pack:
Proven Positive Parenting Tips for Improving Kid's Fitness and Children's Behavior

22. T Raising Teenagers to Choose Wisely:
Keeping your Teen Secure in a Big World

23. Tips for #CollegeLife:
Powerful College Advice for Excelling as a College Freshman

Other Books You'll Love!

24. The Career Success Formula:
Proven Career Development Advice and Finding Rewarding Employment for Young Adults and College Graduates

25. The Motivated Young Adult's Guide to Career Success and Adulthood:
Proven Tips for Becoming a Mature Adult, Starting a Rewarding Career, and Finding Life Balance

26. Bedtime Stories for Kids:
Short Funny Stories and poems Collection for Children and Toddlers

27. Guide for Boarding School Life

28. The Fear of The Lord:
How God's Honour Guarantees Your Peace

Audiobooks

Are available at any of the following retailers:

1.Kobo
https://www.kobo.com/us/en/audiobook/spelling-two-2

2.Google Store
https://play.google.com/store/audiobooks/details/Bukky_Ekine_Ogunlana_Spelling_Two?id=AQAAAEAieyE7EM

3. Libro
https://libro.fm/audiobooks/9798368976426

4.Storytel
https://www.storytel.com/se/sv/books/4261957

5.Scribd
https://www.scribd.com/audiobook/637100295/Spelling-Two-An-Interactive-Vocabulary-and-Spelling-Workbook-for-6-Year-Olds-With-AudioBook-Lessons

6. Audiobooks
https://www.audiobooks.com/audiobook/spelling-two-an-interactive-vocabulary-and-spelling-workbook-for-6-year-olds-with-audiobook-lessons/680176

7. Barnes and Noble
https://www.barnesandnoble.com/w/spelling-two-bukky-ekine-ogunlana/1143328313
8. Spotify
https://open.spotify.com/show/5OA8LA8tMNMiHrwFxRiM60

9. Hoopladigital
https://www.hoopladigital.com/title/16158722

And all other audiobook retailers!

Facebook Community

I invite you to our Facebook community group to visit this link and simply click the join group.

https://www.facebook.com/groups/397683731371863

This is a private group where parents, teachers, and carers can learn, share tips, ask questions, and discuss and get valuable content about raising and parenting modern children.

It is a very supportive and encouraging group where valuable content, free resources, and exciting discussion about parenting are shared. You can use this to benefit from social media.

You will learn a lot from schoolteachers, experts, counselors, and new and experienced parents, and stay updated with our latest releases.

See you there!

Your Free Gift

Your Free Gift!

As a way of saying thank you for Your purchase, I have included a gift that you can download at <u>TCEC publishing .com</u>

References

1. https://www.theseus.fi/bitstream/handle/10024/50239/Anttila_Marianna_Saikkonen_Pinja.pdf

2. https://www.researchgate.net/publication/28372104_Early_Reading_Development

3. https://www2.ed.gov/parents/academic/help/adolescence/adolescence.pdf

4. http://centerforchildwelfare.org/kb/prprouthome/Helping%20Your%20Children%20Navigate%20Their%20Teenage%20Years.pdf

5. https://www.childrensmn.org/images/family_resource_pdf/027121.pdf

6. https://educationnorthwest.org/sites/default/files/developing-empathy-in-children-and-youth.pdf

7. https://www.researchgate.net/publication/263227023_Family_Time_Activities_and_Adolescents'_Emotional_Well-being

8. http://www.delmarlearning.com/companions/content/1418019224/AdditionalSupport/box11.1.pdf

9. https://exeter.anglican.org/wp-content/uploads/2014/11/Listening-to-children-leaflet_NCB.pdf

10. https://www.researchgate.net/publication/312600262_Creative_Thinking_among_Preschool_Children

Made in the USA
Monee, IL
07 October 2023

44118786R00066